Jane Begley is passionate about the natural world and how we must strive to protect it in every way we can. She believes we must take time to reconnect to nature and ourselves, to be ourselves and appreciate the world as a whole! If we put down our phones and computers sometimes and just listen and look at the world, we will be happier with ourselves and enjoy life more.

Jane Begley enjoys writing poems about the world and life, and this is her third book. Her poems are written in a unique style which makes them easy to read and understand.

I dedicate this book to my family who are my support.

Jane Begley

THE LIGHT OF THE WORLD

AUSTIN MACAULEY PUBLISHERS™

LONDON · CAMBRIDGE · NEW YORK · SHARJAH

Copyright © Jane Begley 2023

The right of Jane Begley to be identified as author of this work has been asserted by the author in accordance with sections 77 and 78 of the Copyright, Designs and Patents Act 1988.

All rights reserved. No part of this publication may be reproduced, stored in a retrieval system, or transmitted in any form or by any means, electronic, mechanical, photocopying, recording, or otherwise, without the prior permission of the publishers.

Any person who commits any unauthorised act in relation to this publication may be liable to criminal prosecution and civil claims for damages.

A CIP catalogue record for this title is available from the British Library.

ISBN 9781398480667 (Paperback)
ISBN 9781398480674 (ePub e-book)

www.austinmacauley.com

First Published 2023
Austin Macauley Publishers Ltd®
1 Canada Square
Canary Wharf
London
E14 5AA

The Light of the World

In summer the place where we live is full of light
The sun is upon us and close to us bringing us energy
Everywhere there is abundant growth
Plants and animals alike are multiplying
People are more active and feel more energy
They want to be outside and feel the freedom
They make plans for the future and feel happier
The light from the sun feeds us and feeds the earth.

As the earth moves and we get less sun and light
There is a slowing down of growth and energy
Until when winter is upon us the growing stops
The plants and the animals remain dormant
We spend less time outside and have less light
Our energy recedes and our bodies rest
Then as the light from the sun gets nearer again
Everywhere slowly awakens and begins to grow again.

The world is a finely tuned balance of light and shade
Each and every part of the world is unique to its own balance
As each part of the world has a different balance of light and shade
Our bodies adjust to this light and shade wherever we are born

If we move to another part of the world, our bodies and our souls
Need time to adjust and to feel at peace with where they are
The world is continually adjusting to all that is happening too
Above and below the earth all that we destroy and take from within.

No wonder there are earthquakes, tsunamis and storms.

Listening to the World

The world has many sounds
There is always something somewhere
Moving and making some kind of sound
Life is always on the move, even our heart makes a sound
All around us and inside us there is sound
There is sound in the air
As the wind blows, as it moves through the sky
There is sound coming from the earth
As life emerges from the ground
There are creatures within the earth
Moving around and communicating with each other
There are creatures living on top of the earth
All with their unique ways of communicating
Above the earth the weather patterns are apparent
Rain and wind both gentle and wild
Changing direction and intensity at a whim
These in turn change the sounds of the earth
Feeding and nourishing the life from within
What a unique and diverse world we live in.

The Ground Beneath Us

The ground beneath us is slowly but surely being covered
Covered with buildings and roads, nothing can grow
There are huge areas covered in concrete
Too much concrete can upset the balance of the earth
Too much concrete and people also become unbalanced
The earth is a living and breathing world
And people need to be connected to the earth.

Protecting the World

It is hard to imagine what a unique and amazing world we live in
The only planet with life in a vast universe with so many other planets
It slowly moves so that every part of it is exposed to the sun
Around the world are layers of protection
Making sure its balance is stable and secure.

If we do not look after this precious world
If we do not take the trouble to protect this balance
If we are too greedy and take too much
If we make decisions without considering the bigger picture
The damage we cause will one day be too much
The balance will be lost forever.

Instinct

Every living creature is born with instinct
Babies instinctively know that they are hungry
They instinctively know what to do and when to do it
They watch and listen and learn how to behave
Every living creature instinctively knows what to do
It watches and listens and knows how to behave
Every plant or tree instinctively knows what to do
It feels that its roots need to grow down into the earth
It feels that it must grow up to the light
Birds know when they must migrate and where they must go
As do the fish in the sea and the fish in the rivers
Perhaps we have lost some of our instinctiveness
We somehow have lost the way to behave
We have stopped listening to our hearts
And started listening only to what we are told.

A Word Without Love

Love is our reason for being here on earth
Without love the world could not exist
Without love we would be as savages
Existing only to take what we wanted
Caring nothing for each other or the world.

To feel love and to be touched by love
Is what we all need to be happy
To sit by the sea and to be calm
To feel the sun warming on your face
To feel invigorated after a walk in the fresh air.

All these things are essential to our being
To have a purpose in life, a reason to live
A place to come home to that feels right
Enough money to live a comfortable life
People and family that we love and who care.

If only we could all experience these pleasures
If only we could all be aware of these pleasures
Take some time to feel love for each other
Take some time to appreciate the beauty of the earth
Then the world would be as happy as us.

Within Us

Within each one of us there is a soul
Within each one of us there is a spirit
These are what make us unique and different
These are what make us who we are
If we listen to our feelings
If we listen to our heart
We can be who we are meant to be
If we become who we are meant to be
Our spirit will be happy and we will thrive
We will grow and expand and life will be good
Our enthusiasm will shine and so will we
This enthusiasm will affect those we meet
This enthusiasm will allow others to grow
They will see things that they could not see before
Their hearts and souls will be touched.

The Sky at Night

On a clear summer's night
When the sun is about to disappear
Slowly sinking lower and lower
When the sky is full of amazing colour
We watch in awe as it slowly disappears
When darkness is upon us and a calm descends
Everywhere is still and everywhere is quiet
Only the stars to light up the sky
So many stars are hard to understand
So far away and invisible by day
What an amazing world we live in
What beauty there is to be seen.

The World and All Its People

There are so many people in the world
It is difficult to imagine how they all came to be here
How can the world go on accommodating so many people?
Every minute of every day a new life comes into being
Why do some people insist on having so many children?
We are all living longer but not necessarily in a healthy way
It is too easy to sit around and let someone else care for you
It is much nicer to stay active and alert, never feeling that you are old
Taking responsibility for your own life until the end
Enjoying your life on this beautiful planet
Sensing the things that make you happy
Never giving in and never giving up
Instead of arguing and fighting
Instead of bickering and complaining
Why not embrace the good things
And make the most of your precious time on earth.

Seeing from Within

Seeing from within is a kind of feeling
A feeling that things are not as they seem
They may look right on the outside
But there is something that is not quite right
If we register this feeling and hold on to it
Sooner or later, we will know what is not as it seems
Sometimes it is the people that we know
Sometimes the places that we visit
We may go into a building that just doesn't feel good
It could be the energy from beneath
It could be the people that have lived there
It could even be something that has happened there
If we do not acknowledge these feelings
If we do not take note of these feelings
We may make the wrong decision at the wrong time
Not listening to these feelings is not listening to our soul
Our soul is the guider of our life on earth.

Inside the Earth

Inside the earth there is so much happening
Areas that are constantly moving, constantly changing
The earth moves and buildings are destroyed
Even beneath the sea the earth moves
Causing the sea to erupt with huge waves
Waves so big they destroy everything in their way.

Inside the earth there are massive fires burning
Some hidden deep inside smouldering away
The pressure builds and builds until the earth explodes
Sending fire and molten rocks high into the sky
Everything in its path is burnt and destroyed
It is nature's way of keeping the balance of the earth.

The earth is a living, breathing, finely balanced planet
We must take care that we do not upset this balance.

The Pressures of Life

Life is full of pressures to succeed
The pressure begins when we are at school
We are compared to our peers by our parents and teachers
We are different and we develop in different ways
Some of us develop quickly and others take longer
Why is it that the world expects us to all be the same?
If we were all the same, we would all want the same jobs
There would be no variety in life, no enjoyment or fun
Unfortunately, if we do not reach a certain standard at school
If we do not conform to the norm, we are deemed to have failed
Which is not at all easy for a teenager to understand
Someone who has other gifts to be explored
The world is a unique and diverse place
Full of unique and diverse people
If we do not take the time to encourage young people
To show them some time to explore their gifts
They will become disheartened with life
Some of them turn to crime and some to radicalisation
Let us spend more time with the future generations
Allowing them to grow into who they are supposed to be.

The Beauty of Life

We are lucky enough to have television and films
Where we can see all the amazing parts of the world
Some of us are lucky enough to visit them too
To wonder and admire such awesome sights
Do these amazing sights make us more aware
Do they make us want to look after the world
Or do we just forget what we have seen
Do we just carry on as before without being aware
Aware of the beauty around us without a thought
Our life here is short and it is up to us to do our bit
To give a little bit of love to our beautiful world.

Will the World Become a Peaceful Place?

A place where we can all live peacefully
Where countries decide to live side by side
Concentrating on their own land and people
Instead of fighting with their neighbours
What is it they are fighting for?
Are they fighting for more land?
Are they fighting to stay alive
Or are they so discontent with life
That they want to destroy the life of others
Is this what we have evolved to become
Or have we just turned full circle
Have we become like savages again?

If only these people would look at what they want to become
Would they not prefer to be loved and to love?
Would they not like to be happy and content
With a nice place to live and a family to take care of
To see the world as a beautiful place
To marvel at the uniqueness of the world
To wonder at how we came to be here
Can they not look at the people who live here?
Can they not see they are just trying to do their best
Wanting a better life for themselves and their children

A life that is peaceful and a life to enjoy
How wonderful if we could all live side by side in peace.

The World at Night

How different everything appears in the dark
Everything feels so different and even a little scary
Especially away from people and houses
The world is silent and everything is still
The few sounds to be heard are loud and echo
The world appears to have gone to sleep.

If you live on your own, you feel more lonely at night
There are fewer people out and about and less traffic
There is no one to talk to or communicate with
Our senses are heightened with the stillness around
Feelings of fear and pain are worse at night
Panic can easily take over from calm and sense.

When there are no distractions from our normal life
Our thoughts can run riot and appear out of control
We think of the past and all the bad things that have happened
Instead of the people we love and the good things we have
Doing something like making a cup of tea
Can change the moment and stop the panic
How strange it is that everything appears different at night.

Energy

We cannot see energy
We can only feel energy
We feel energy in our bodies
We feel energy in the air
We feel energised when we are walking
We feel energised when we are happy
We feel energised when we have a purpose
When we know where we are heading
When we are stimulated by our passion
When everything feels right
When we have love in our lives
Then we can feel and see the energy of life.

Happiness

Happiness is sought the whole world over
If everyone was happy what would the world be like
If only we could all work towards being happy
If only we knew what to do and how to do it
If we started by finding little things that we enjoy
Ways of feeling good about ourselves
Good about the way we look
Feeling fit and healthy too
Perhaps then the rest would follow
Something to work towards and something to achieve
If everyone all over the world made an effort to be happy
Instead of complaining and fighting amongst ourselves
We could work together to make the world a happy place to be.

All Around Us

All around us life is going on
Nothing is ever still, something is always moving
People all over the world are going about their lives
The ground is constantly moving, plants and trees
Animals and insects and birds moving too
The world itself is slowly moving, changing seasons
Even while we are asleep our bodies are living and breathing
Creating movement, creating energy, creating life.

Our lives too are constantly moving
As we grow older everything changes
We are constantly growing, constantly learning
Learning about the world, learning about ourselves
Our brain is forever changing, as we look and listen
Holding on to some information and letting go of some
Listening to our heart and soul, telling us which way to go
How amazing is life, how amazing are we!

The Earth Beneath Us

The earth is full of amazing wonders
Rich in minerals and precious stones
Compressed by the changing earth
Preserved over millions of years
The earth contains everything needed
For life on earth to exist forever.

Why is it then that we are trying to destroy it?
Why do we use bombs to blow it up?
Why do we use nuclear power?
A power that destroys everything and more
A power that poisons the earth for centuries untold
A poison that could tip the balance of the earth.

Are people so stupid that they cannot see
What a highly dangerous substance it is
Even after evidence of several disasters
They are willing to risk all for ease or power
What will it take for sense to prevail?
The earth contains all that we need to live.

Bringing the World Together

How long will it take for the world to unite?
How is it that the wrong people end up in power?
Power that they use to manipulate mankind
What kind of mentality has brought them to believe
That power and cruelty can win over Love
Those that use power over love
Will always crumble and die
In the whole history of the world
Evil has always been destroyed
Still, it seems we have not learnt from this
Still, it seems there are people who feel superior
They feel it is their right to control and destroy
They see only what they want to see
They are not connected to themselves or the world
They do not see the love or the beauty they are destroying
Such people must not be allowed to continue
Or the world will never be united together.

The World Is a Mess

Is it possible for the world to come together
To work as a team for the good of all
There are so many different cultures and beliefs
People are unwilling to let go of
Beliefs which have helped to keep people together
But now they are tearing them apart
Perhaps if they were to come together
They could make a list of common beliefs
For the benefit of all mankind and to help protect the world
A decent life for everyone with hope and love and awareness
Surely everyone alive would love just to be happy.

Upsetting the Balance

What would happen if we upset the balance of the world?
If the earth cannot breathe as it should
If we extract too much of everything from it
Leaving holes which cannot be filled again
If we build and build covering it with concrete
If we cut down huge areas of trees and leave it bare
Trees that help us to breathe and clean the air
And we continue to pollute the air with chemicals
How long will it be before it begins to die?
Before it starts to move and tilt
Before there is no turning back
Then the world will start to die
Then the people will be no more.

Whatever Happened to Love

If we can love and understand
If we can see inside our hearts
And be aware of how others feel
Be aware of another's anxieties
Know when and when not to speak
Then we can be happy and content.

If we truly love someone
We can sense what they are feeling
We can give them space when they need it
And know when they are angry or unhappy
Be aware of whether they need comfort or time
To express how and what they are feeling.

Life is not always straightforward or clear
It is often difficult to know what to do
To expose our feelings is not always appropriate
Sometimes it is better to wait and see
Life usually has a way of sorting things out
Then we can be happy and content once again.

Nature and Love

If we cannot enjoy nature, we cannot feel love
If we are not aware of the beauty of nature
Our energy will wilt and eventually die
Nature feeds us and feeds the world
It calms the soul and energises our heart
It gives us the will to be who we are
It gives us the power to want to succeed
If only the world could see how necessary
How absolutely essential it is to preserve
Nature and to love what we came here to do.

Good Things Are Coming

Sometimes it is hard to see how anything can get any better
Life is complicated and not always straightforward
Not knowing where you are going or how to get there
Feeling trapped in a life that is not what you want
You know what you want but not how to find it.

You just want to be happy and do what you want
You just want someone to love you and someone to love
Somewhere nice to live and somewhere that feels right
To go out and about and to see more of the world
To do some of the things you have longed to do.

With someone who cares in the same way you do.

Repairing Our World

We are told it is not too late to repair the world
If we put back all that we have taken
If we use only renewable sources
If we re-use all the bad things we have made
The metal and plastic and wood and glass
If we invest in the future and not in the now
If governments would only have the courage
To explore and to listen to what they know is right
Instead of seeing only what is in front of them
There are SO many people who have all the answers
If only governments would explore them all
It is better to take some time and get it right
Than to take the easy way out!

The World's Pandemic

We have and still are in the grip of a world pandemic
We have been stopped in our tracks
We have been forced to stay at home
We have had time to reflect and wonder why
Why has this terrible thing happened?
We are a world full of technology and yet…
We cannot stop the spread of this virus
A virus which we have caused to exist
We have invaded the natural world to excess
We have caused pain and suffering to wild animals
We have listened only to what someone has told us
We have not respected life on this beautiful planet.

A Wake-Up Call

Surely this pandemic is a message to us all
Life does not just exist for us alone
We are part of an ecosystem
If we destroy any of it, the rest does not work
We are here for a reason
We are here to make sure everything stays as it should
Common sense is all it takes
Why do we make everything so complicated?
How did we get to a point where we cannot function
Without mobile phones, the Internet and social media
We also need a balance, just like the world
So let us get back to nature and enjoy it.

Without the World

We cannot survive without the world
All the technology in the world cannot help
It is one of the reasons it is all going wrong
We are not connected to the world we live in
We are not connected to ourselves
We are not aware of our surroundings
We are not aware of different energy
We are not present in the now.

We must protect and respect the world
We must make sure the world we live in
Is repaired and put back together with love
Let us all work together as one nation
To find a way to restore the balance
Instead of arguing, we must find a way
In every part of the world people are working
Working to restore the balance of the world.

Forever Young

Always love just who you are
And be yourself wherever you are
Never try to be someone else
You are meant to be just who you are
There are times when you are sad
There are times when you are happy
Life brings us all lots of ups and downs
But always love just who you are.

Ingram Content Group UK Ltd.
Milton Keynes UK
UKHW021514220623
423876UK00009B/165